Today's Chords
And How To Use Them
for all keyboards

Order No. NM10000
International Standard Book Number: 0.8256.4225.6

Exclusive Distributors:
Music Sales Corporation
257 Park Avenue South, New York, NY 10010 USA
Music Sales Limited
8/9 Frith Street, London W1D 3JB England
Music Sales Pty. Limited
120 Rothschild Street, Rosebery, Sydney, NSW 2018, Australia

Printed in the United States of America by
Vicks Lithograph and Printing Corporation

Nancy Music Company, Inc.
New York, New York

PREFACE

This book is about New Sounding Chords and how to learn and play them rather quickly on a keyboard instrument.

The chords discussed have a beautiful Debussy-like quality. Therefore, it should be relatively easy for the student to remember each one's distinctive sound.

I suggest once you've learned an exercise, practice with your eyes closed.

Learn to listen! Program your mind to memorize the sound and the notes of each new chord, then adapt it into your own style of playing.

Remember: *Learn to listen, practice and analyze!*

Good Luck!

MAJOR 7th CHORDS

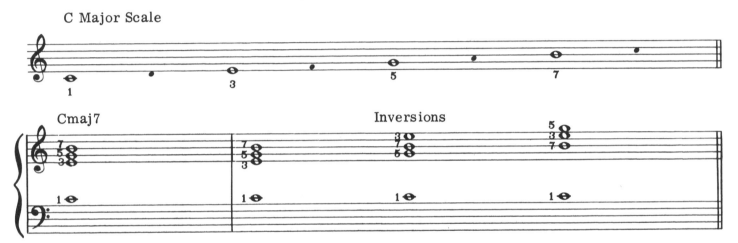

A major 7th is a marvelous chord that has a beautiful, distinctive sound. It is constructed from the 1-3-5-7 scale steps of a major scale. Cmaj7 1-3-5-7 scale steps of a C major scale C-E-G-B.

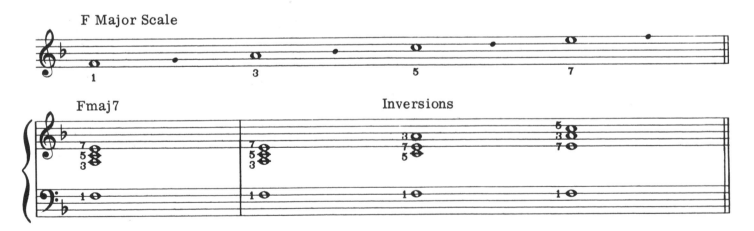

An F major 7th chord is constructed from the 1-3-5-7 scale steps of an F major scale F-A-C-E, etc.

LISTEN TO THE DIFFERENCE BETWEEN THIS SOUND:

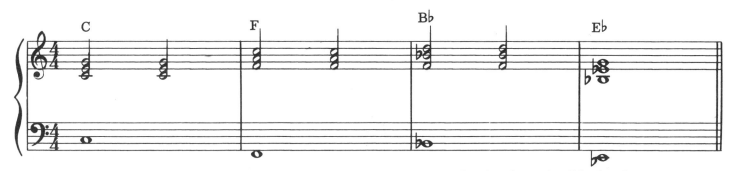

Notice the difference between the sound of a major chord and a major 7th chord.

AND THIS SOUND!

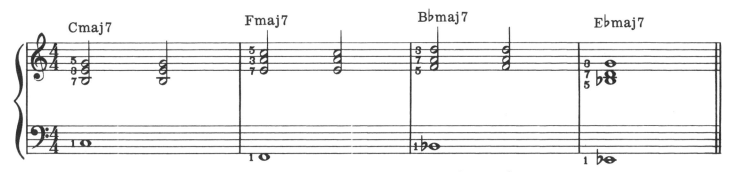

The major 7th adds a new dimension to the sound.

LISTEN TO THE DIFFERENCE BETWEEN THIS SOUND:

AND THIS SOUND!

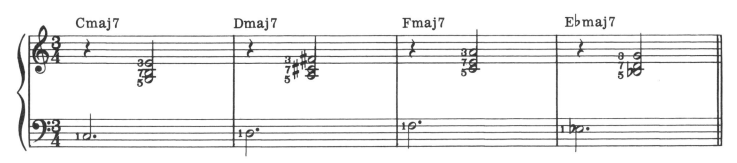

NOTE: It is impossible to describe the sound of a chord. To obtain the exact shade of meaning, sit down and play, and listen!

THE KEY TO LEARNING CHORDS:

KNOW THE MAJOR SCALES!

* **A major 7th chord is constructed from the 1-3-5-7 scale steps of a major scale.**

MAJOR 7th CHORD EXAMPLES

MAJOR 7th INVERSIONS

INVERSIONS
MAJOR 7TH CHORDS

INVERSIONS
MAJOR 7TH CHORDS

MAJOR 7th INVERSION EXAMPLES

NOTE: Program your mind to memorize the sound and the notes of each new chord.

7 - 6 RESOLUTION

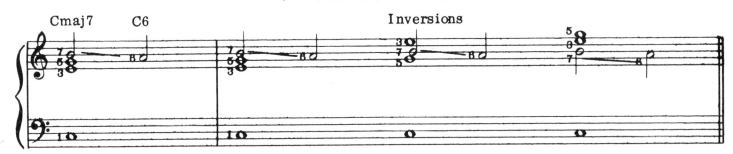

The chord tone 7th resolves normally to chord tone 6 (7-6). This resolution relieves the tension created by the major 7th and also adds a beautiful natural movement within the chord.

LISTEN TO THE DIFFERENCE BETWEEN THIS SOUND:

AND THIS SOUND!

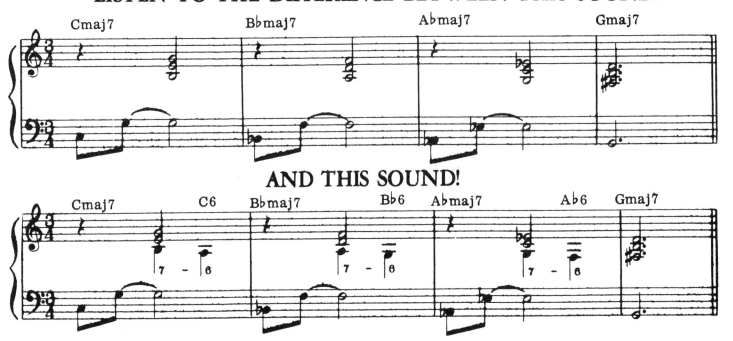

THE DIFFERENCE BETWEEN THIS SOUND:

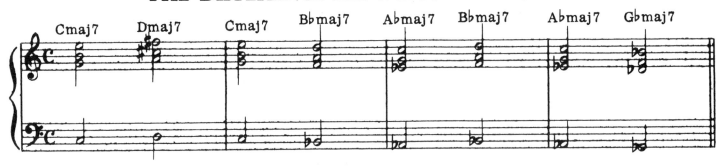

AND THIS SOUND!

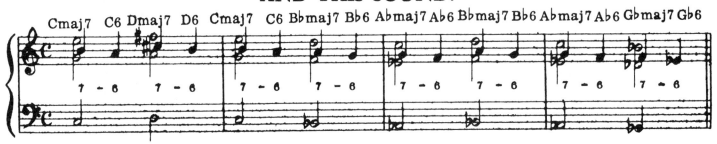

LISTEN TO THE DIFFERENCE BETWEEN THIS SOUND:

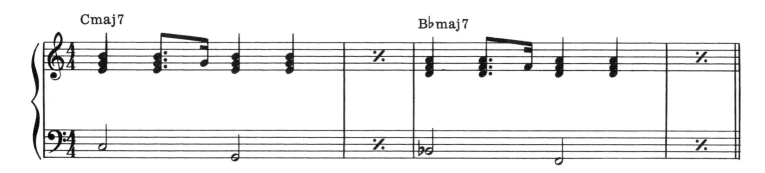

AND THIS SOUND!

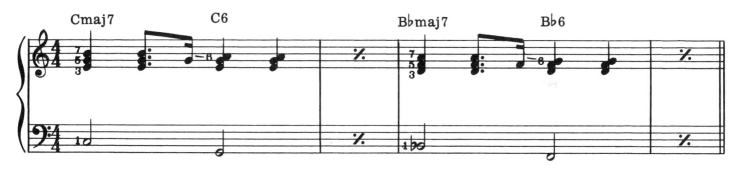

THIS SOUND:

AND THIS SOUND!

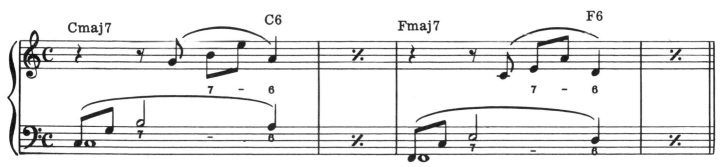

7 - 6 EXAMPLES

7 - 6 INVERSIONS

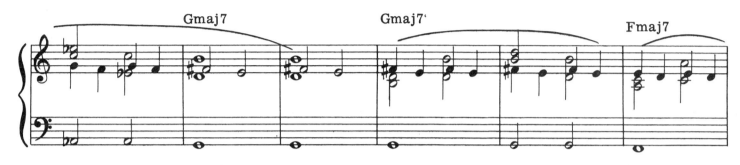

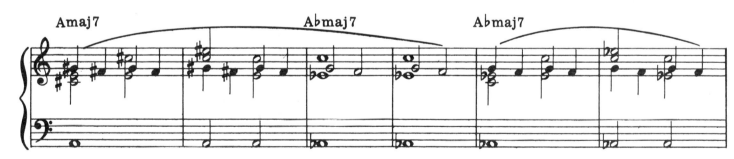

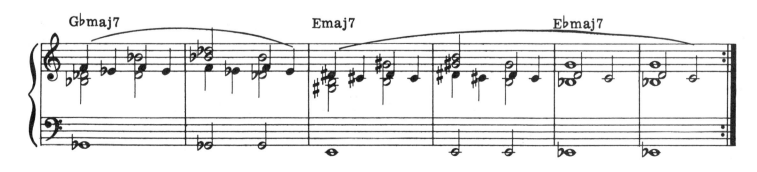

7 - 6 INVERSION EXAMPLES

*NOTE: Notice in this voicing the chord tone 5th is omitted without any apparent change in sound.

Remember: *Practice, listen, and analyze!*

7 - 1 RESOLUTION

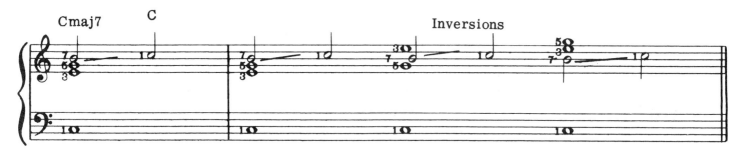

The resolution of the major 7th to 1 (7-1) is a beautiful sound, both harmonically and melodically.

LISTEN TO THE DIFFERENCE BETWEEN THIS SOUND:

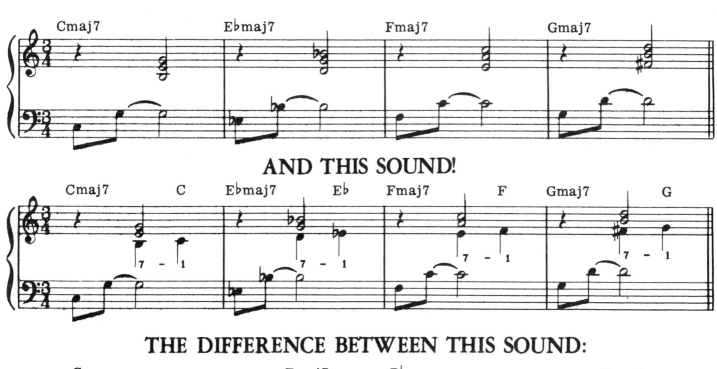

AND THIS SOUND!

THE DIFFERENCE BETWEEN THIS SOUND:

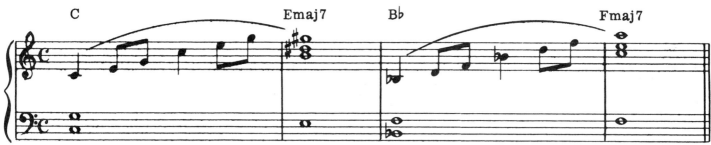

AND THIS SOUND!

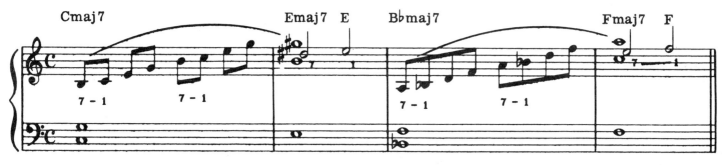

7 - 1 INVERSIONS

7 - 1, 4 - 3 EXAMPLES

INVERSIONS
MAJOR 6TH/ MAJOR 7TH CHORDS

INVERSIONS
MAJOR 6TH/ MAJOR 7TH CHORDS

THE KEY TO LEARNING CHORDS:

KNOW THE MAJOR SCALES!

Learn to listen!

ADDED 9th CHORD EXAMPLES

Learn to listen, practice, and analyze!

ADDED 9th INVERSIONS

Once you've learned an exercise, close your eyes and learn to listen to what your playing—recognize the sounds!

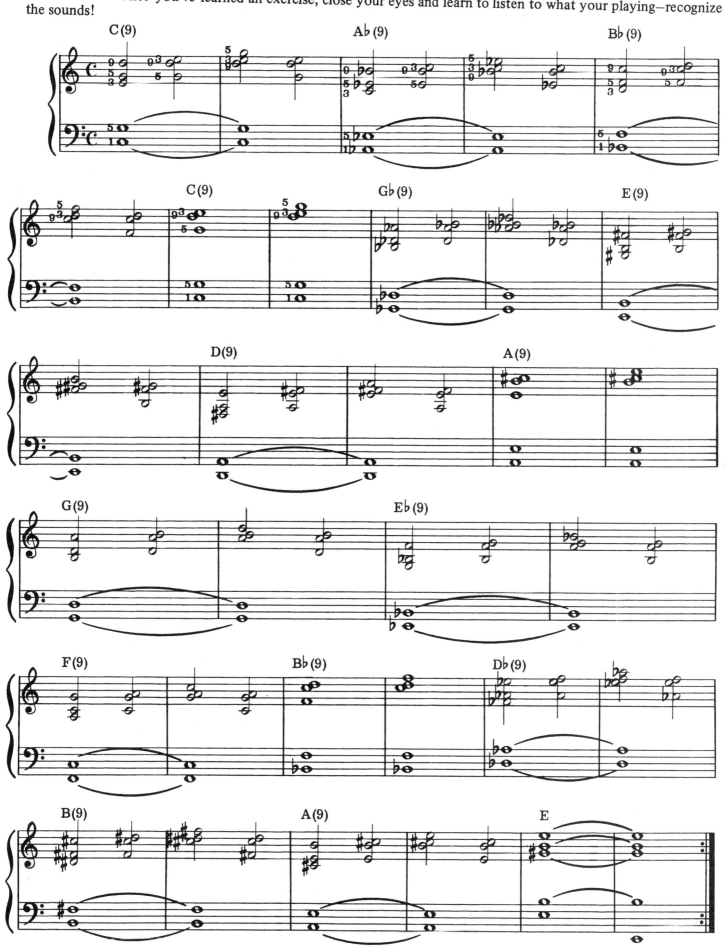

ADDED 9th INVERSION EXAMPLES

Learn to listen, practice, and analyze!

9 - 1 RESOLUTION

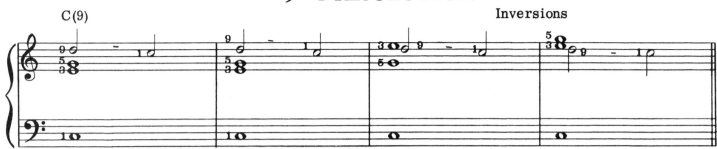

The chord tone 9th resolves normally to chord tone 1 (9-1). This resolution relieves the tension created by the added 9th and also adds a beautiful natural movement within the chord.

LISTEN TO THE DIFFERENCE BETWEEN THIS SOUND:

AND THIS SOUND!

THE DIFFERENCE BETWEEN THIS SOUND:

AND THIS SOUND!

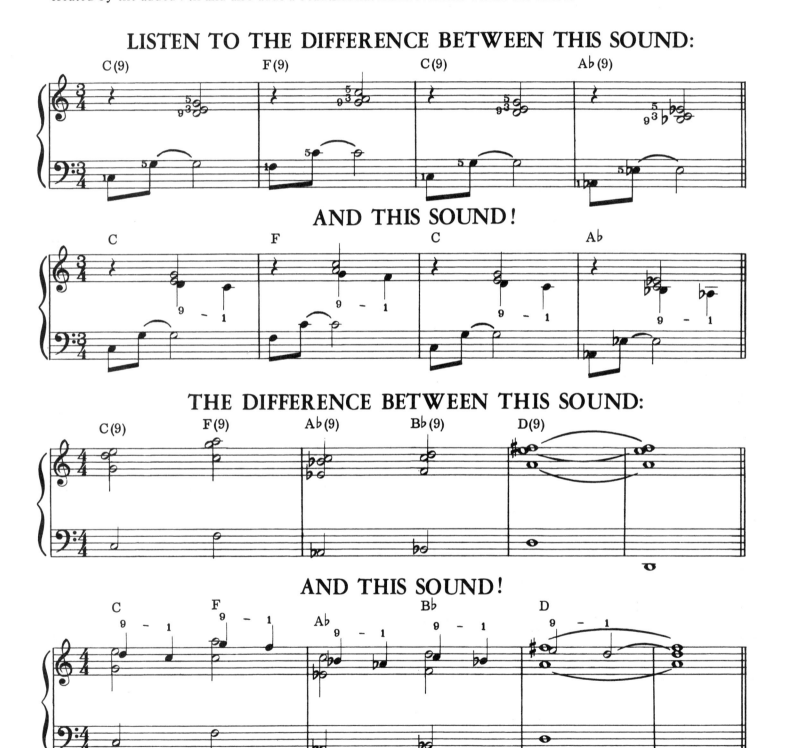

LISTEN TO THE DIFFERENCE BETWEEN THIS SOUND:

AND THIS SOUND!

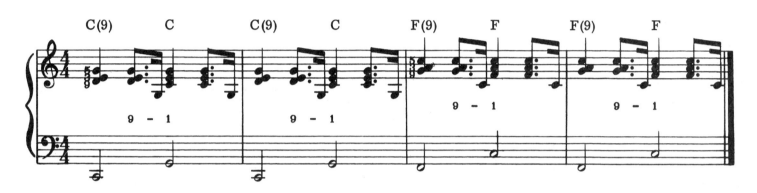

THIS SOUND:

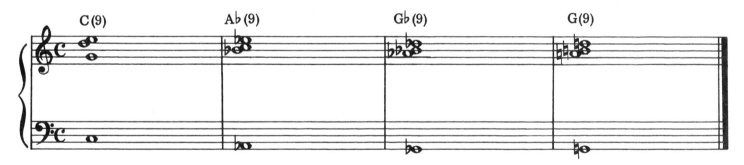

AND THIS SOUND!

9 - 1 EXAMPLES

The 9-1 resolution is a very commercial harmonic device. Learn it in every key!

9 - 1 INVERSIONS

Anyone trying to make it in today's music world has to be well informed. *Learn to listen, practice and analyze!*

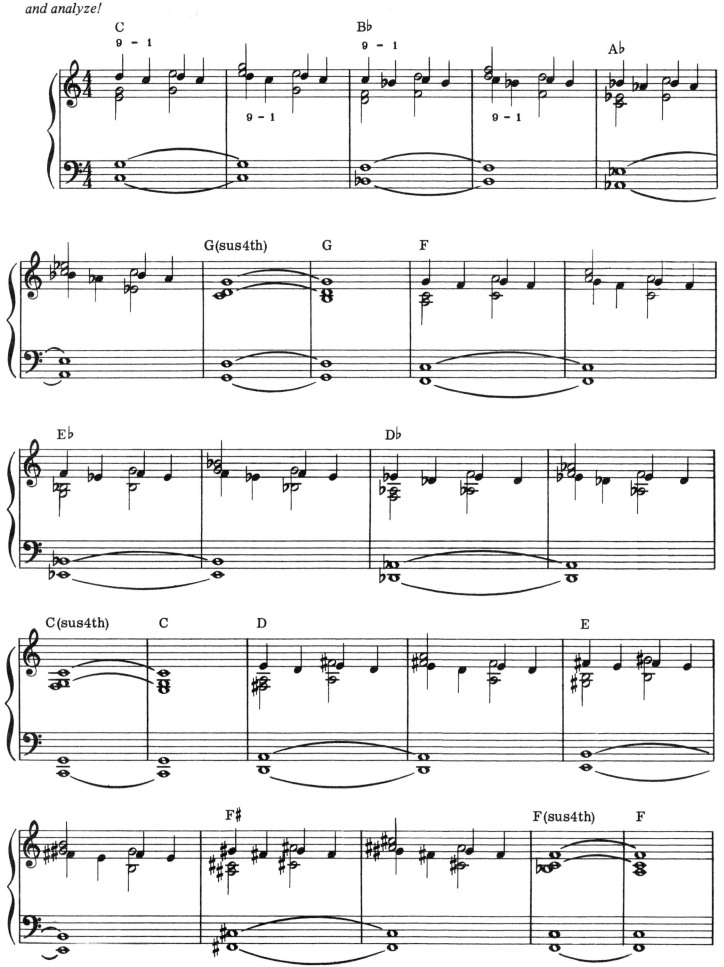

35

36

9 - 1 INVERSION EXAMPLES

9 - 3 RESOLUTION

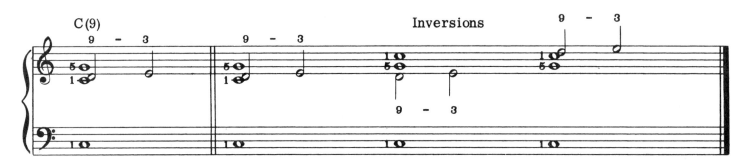

The chord tone 9th also resolves to chord tone 3 (9-3). This is an interesting sound because the 3rd which flavors the chord (either major or minor) is not heard on the initial impact.

LISTEN TO THE DIFFERENCE BETWEEN THIS SOUND:

AND THIS SOUND!

THIS SOUND:

AND THIS SOUND!

9 - 3 INVERSIONS

INVERSIONS
MAJ.6TH WITH THE ADDED 9TH CHORDS

INVERSIONS
MAJ.6TH WITH THE ADDED 9TH CHORDS

SUSPENDED 4th CHORDS

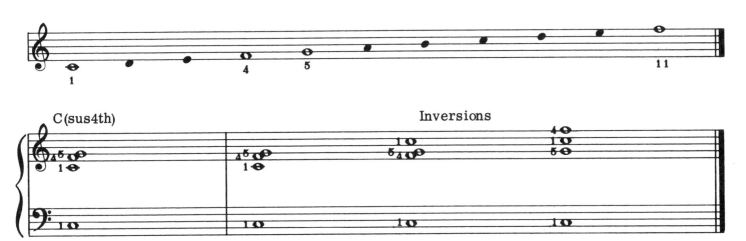

A chord with a suspended 4th (sometimes called an 11th chord) is the most versatile and distinctive of all chords. It is constructed from the 1-4-5 scale steps of a major scale. It uses various chord symbols: C(sus4th); C(susF); C11.

SUSPENDED 4th INVERSIONS

Learn these fantastic sounds in every inversion!

SUSPENDED 4th INVERSION EXAMPLES

48

4 - 3 RESOLUTION

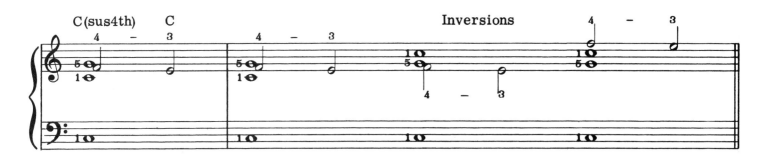

The classic resolution 4-3 is the most magnificent sound in all harmony! Learn to use this resolution in every key and you'll add a new dimension to your musical knowledge.

Learn to listen, practice, and analyze!

4 - 3 EXAMPLES

4 - 3 INVERSIONS

Learn to recognize these sounds in every inversion.

51

9 - 1, 9 - 3, 4 - 3 EXAMPLES

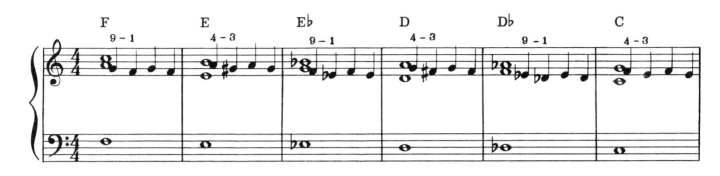

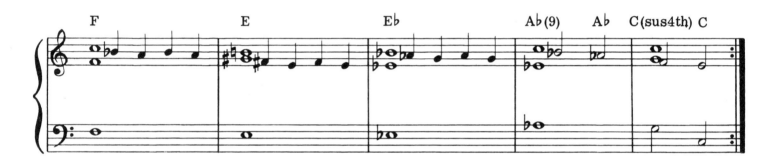

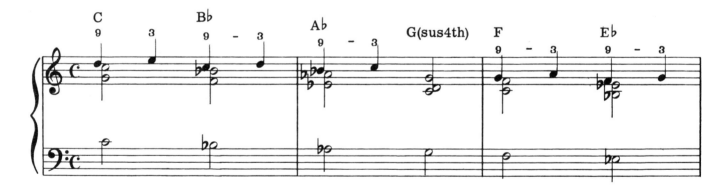

Learn to listen, practice, and analyze!

MAJOR 7th ADDED 9th CHORDS

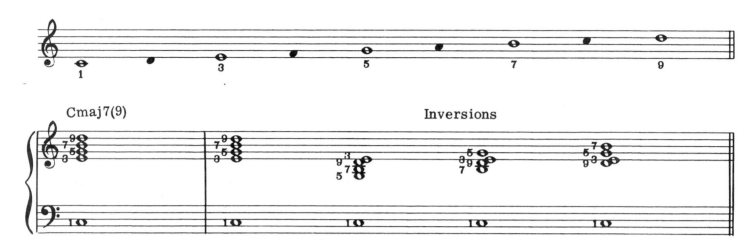

A major 7th with the added 9th chord is constructed from the 1-3-5-7-9 scale steps of a major scale. It is another beautiful sounding chord. Learn to use it in every key.

56

MAJOR 7th (9) INVERSIONS

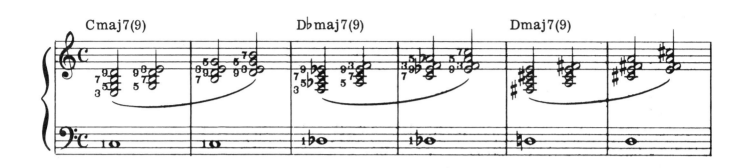

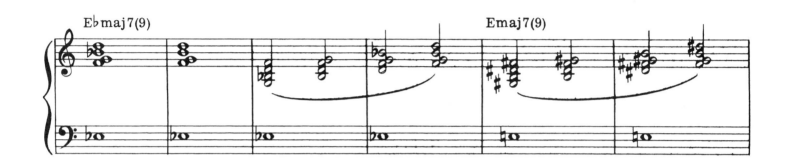

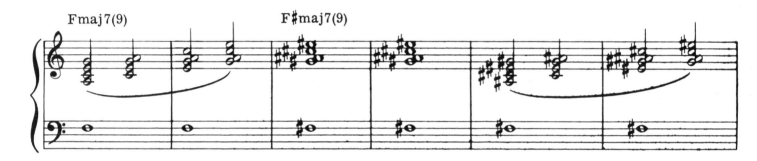

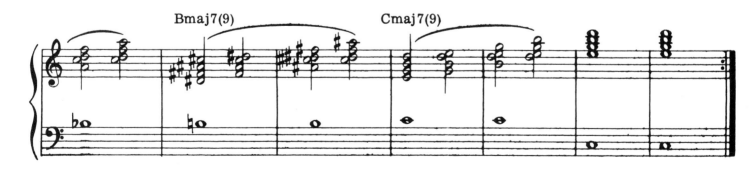

MAJOR 7th ADDED 9th INVERSION EXAMPLES

Learn to listen, practice, and analyze!

58

9 - 1, 7 - 6 RESOLUTION

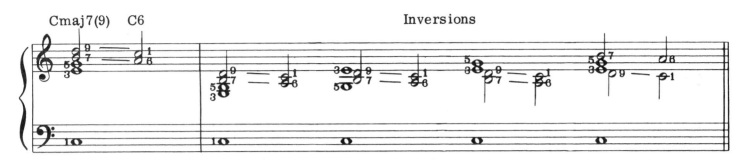

The chord tones 9 and 7 resolve downward to chord tones 1 and 6 respectively (9-1, 7-6). This resolution may appear complex but once learned is very useful.

LISTEN TO THE DIFFERENCE BETWEEN THIS SOUND:

EXAMPLES

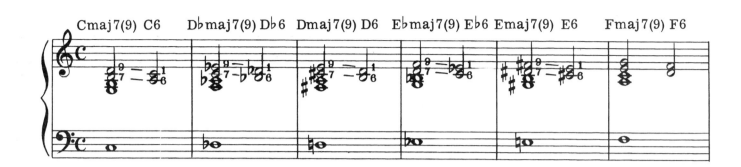

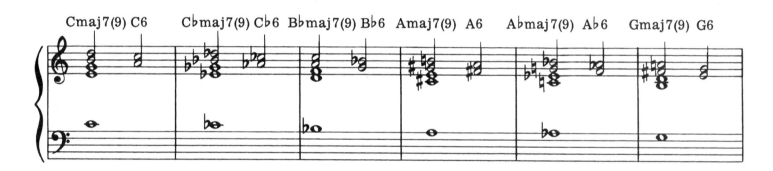

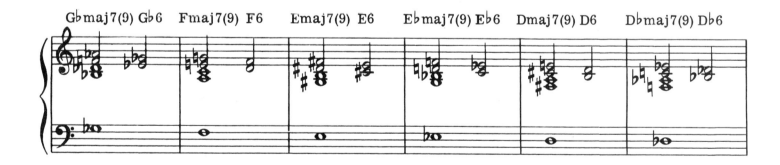

9 - 1, 7 - 6 INVERSIONS

INVERSIONS
MAJ.7TH WITH THE ADDED 9TH CHORDS

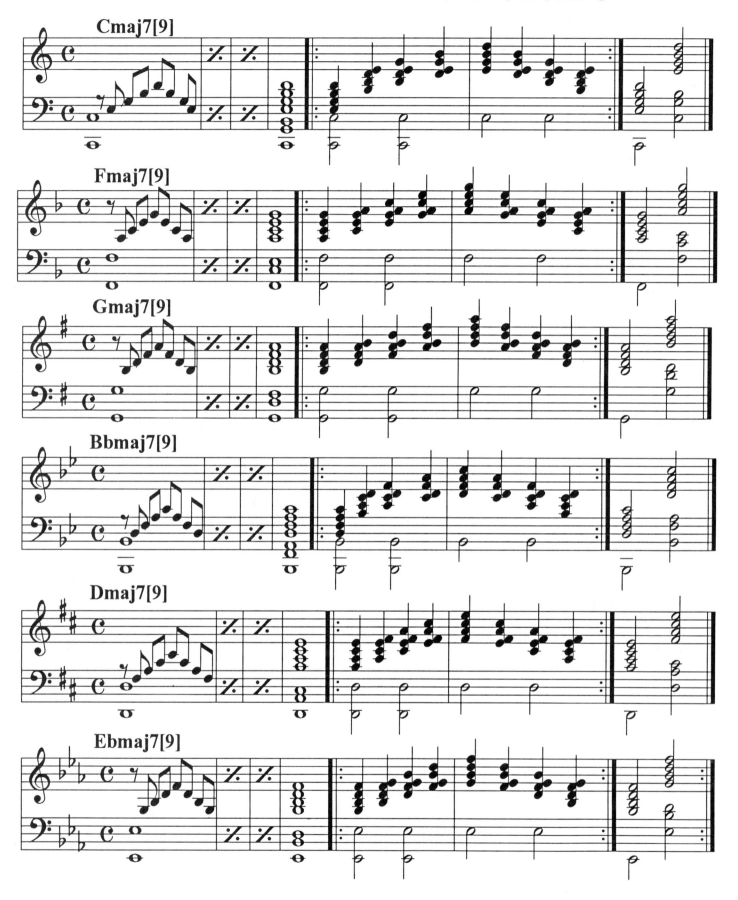

INVERSIONS
MAJ.7TH WITH THE ADDED 9TH CHORDS

MINOR 7th WITH THE ADDED 9th CHORD

Theoretically, a minor 7th with the added 9th chord is obtained by constructing a chord in 3rds on the 2nd scale step of a major scale. It's normal resolution is to a dominant chord a 5th below Dm7(9) to G7.

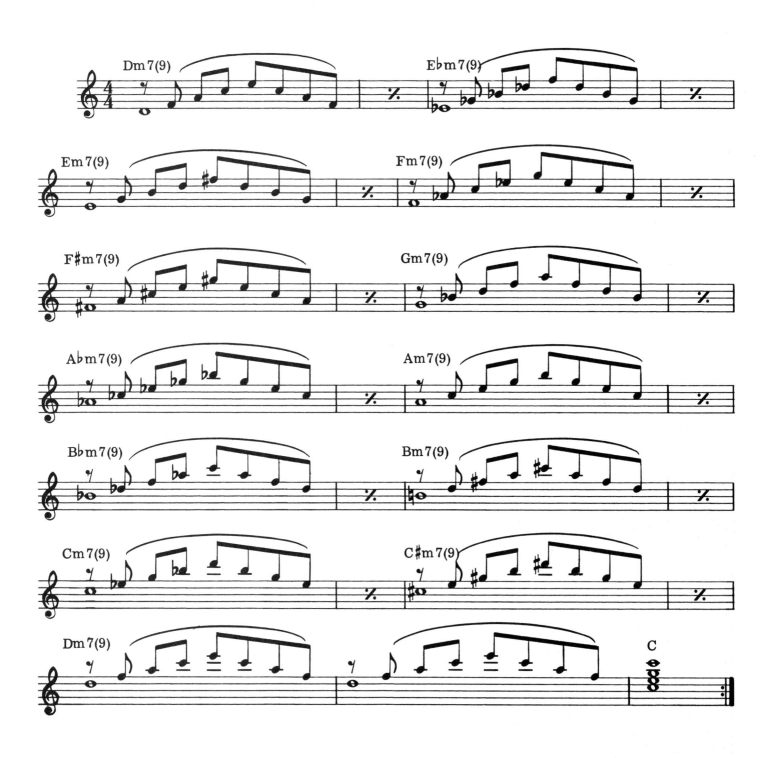

MINOR 7th WITH THE ADDED 9th CHORD

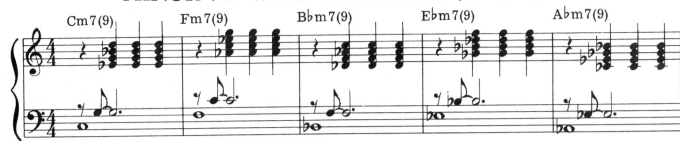

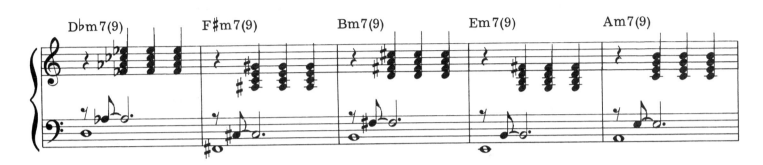

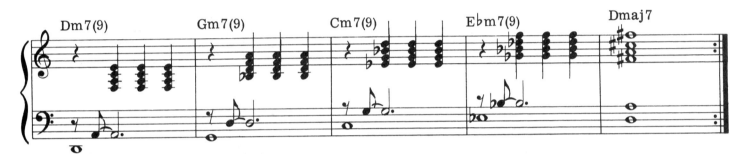

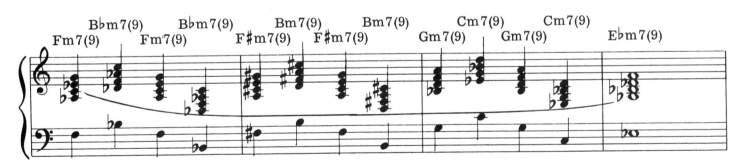

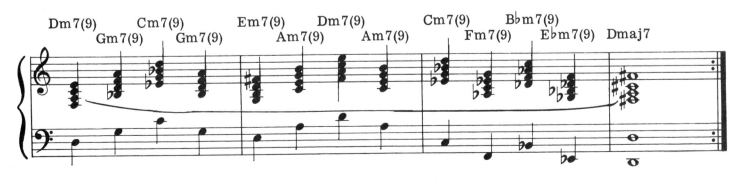

INVERSIONS
MINOR 7TH WITH THE ADDED 9TH CHORDS

INVERSIONS
MINOR 7TH WITH THE ADDED 9TH CHORDS

MINOR 7th ADDED 9th AND 11th CHORDS

This is a magnificent sounding chord! Spend a lot of time learning its sound and note content in every key!

Remember: *Learn to listen!* Program your mind to memorize the sound and the notes of each chord.

11 - b3, 9 - 1 RESOLUTION

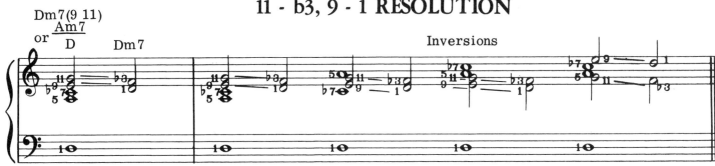

The chord tones 11 and 9 resolve downward to chord tones b3 and 1 respectively (11-b3, 9-1). The chord symbol can be a minor 7th chord whose root is a 5th above the root of the fundamental chord. For a Dm7(9 11) chord use Am7 over D bass. Cm7(9 11) use Gm7 over a C bass, etc.

11 - b3, 9 - 1 INVERSIONS

MINOR CHORDS WITH THE ADDED 9th

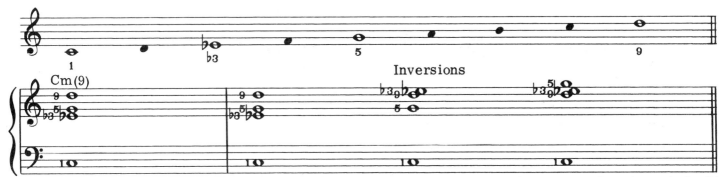

A minor chord with an added 9th can be constructed from the 1-♭3-5-9 steps of a major scale Cm(9) C-E♭-G-D. The treatment of this chord is exactly the same as it was with a major chord with an added 9th. See Book #1, bottom of page 2.

LISTEN TO THE DIFFERENCE BETWEEN THIS SOUND:

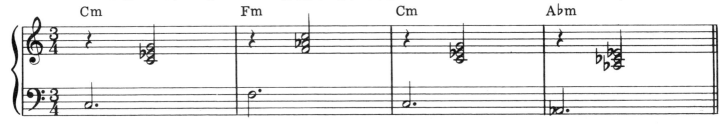

AND THIS SOUND!

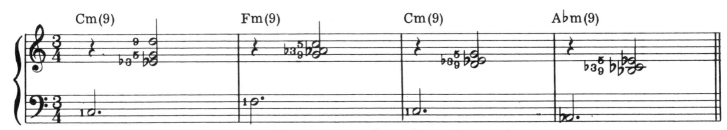

Adding the 9th adds a new dimension to the sound.

THIS SOUND:

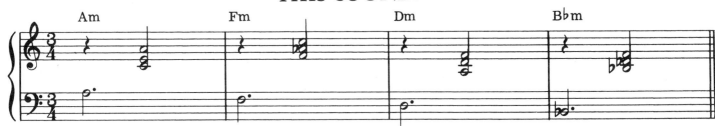

AND THIS SOUND!

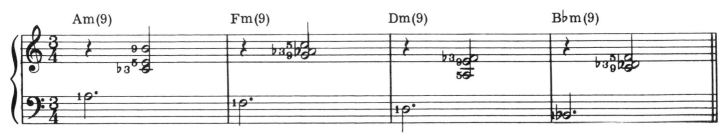

MINOR CHORDS ADDED 9th EXAMPLES

MINOR CHORDS ADDED 9th INVERSIONS

ADDED 9th INVERSION EXAMPLES

Remember: *Practice, listen and analyze!*

9 - 1 RESOLUTION

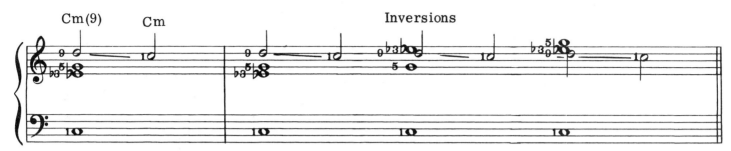

As in the major, the chord tone 9th in a minor chord resolves normally to chord tone 1 (9-1). This resolution relieves the tension created by the added 9th and also adds a beautiful natural movement within the chord.

LISTEN TO THE DIFFERENCE BETWEEN THIS SOUND:

AND THIS SOUND!

THIS SOUND:

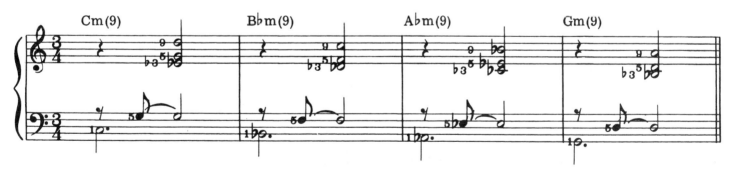

AND THIS SOUND!

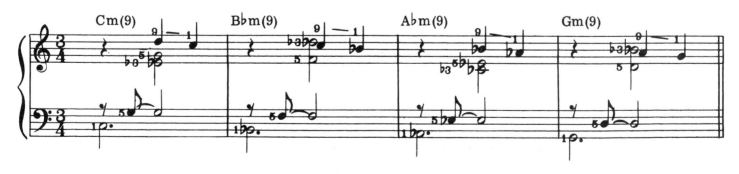

9 - 1 INVERSIONS

9 - b3 RESOLUTION

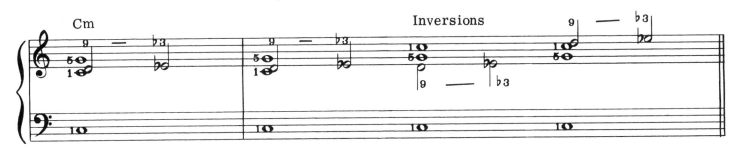

The chord tone 9th also resolves to minor chord tone ♭3 (9-♭3).

LISTEN TO THE DIFFERENCE BETWEEN THIS SOUND:

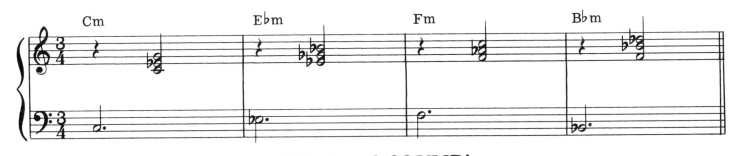

AND THIS SOUND!

THIS SOUND:

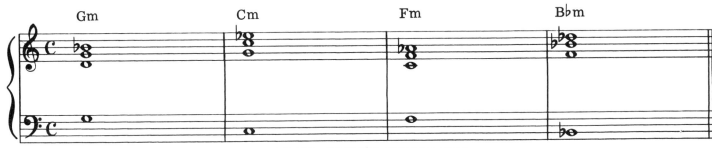

AND THIS SOUND!

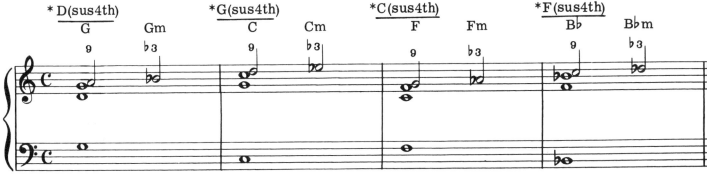

*Note: The chord symbol for this type of resolution (9-♭3) can be a suspended 4th chord whose root (letter name) is a 5th above the root of the fundamental minor chord. The 9- 3 resolution for a G minor chord can be notated D(sus4th) over a G bass. Cmin. (G(sus4th) over a C bass. Fmin. C(sus4th) over an F bass, etc.

9 - b3 INVERSIONS

Remember: *Practice, listen, and analyze!*

4 - b3 RESOLUTION

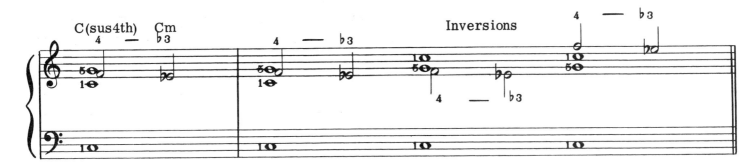

In a minor chord, the chord tone 4th resolves downward to the minor 3rd (4-b3).

4 - b3 INVERSIONS

9 - 1, 9 - b3, 4 - b3 EXAMPLES

DOMINANT 9th CHORD

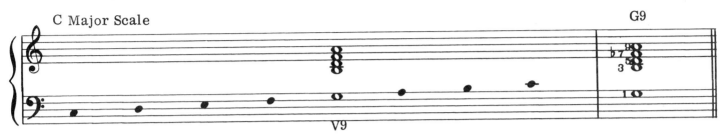

A chord constructed in 3rds on the 5th note of a major scale is called a dominant chord. A dominant 9th chord, as its name infers is a strong, thick sounding chord. Learn its sound and notes in every key!

DOMINANT 9th EXAMPLES

* Note: G Clef

DOMINANT 9th INVERSIONS

Remember: *Learn to listen!* Program your mind to memorize the sound and the notes of each chord.

INVERSIONS
DOMINANT 9TH CHORDS

INVERSIONS
DOMINANT 9TH CHORDS

88

9 - 1 RESOLUTION

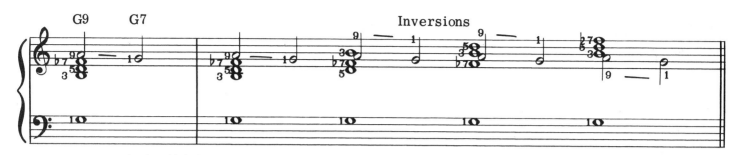

As in all 9-1 resolutions, the chord tone 9th resolves normally to chord tone 1 (9-1). This resolution relieves the tension created by the added 9th and also adds a beautiful natural movement within the chord.

LISTEN TO THE DIFFERENCE BETWEEN THIS SOUND:

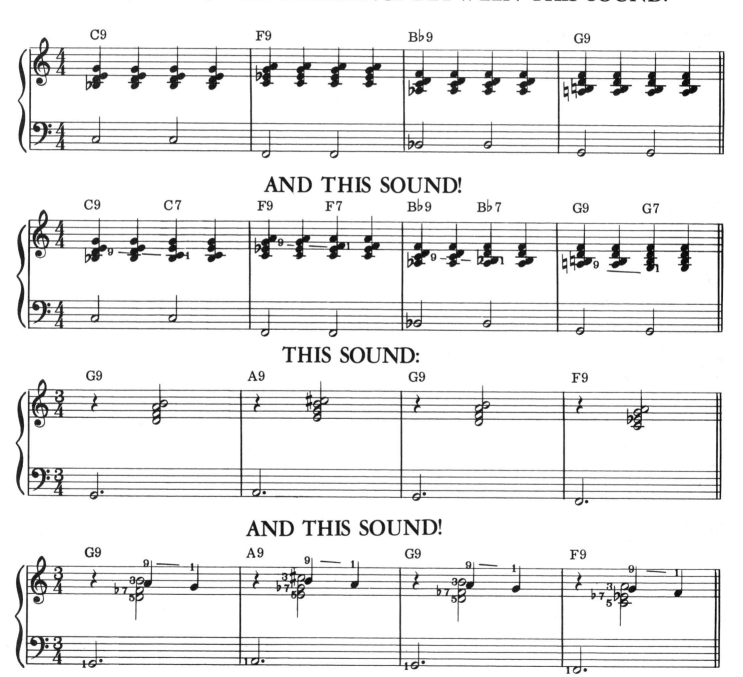

AND THIS SOUND!

THIS SOUND:

AND THIS SOUND!

9 - 1 EXAMPLES

9 - 1 INVERSIONS

DOMINANT 7th WITH A FLAT 9th CHORD

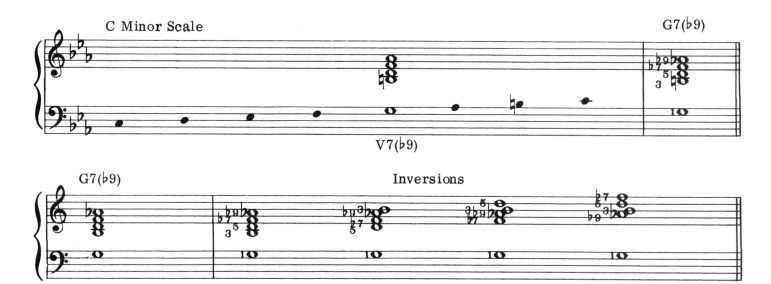

A chord constructed in thirds on the 5th scale step of a minor scale is called a dominant chord. The flat 9th flavors this chord with a moody sensuous sound. Its normal resolution is to a minor chord a 5th below. (G7(♭9) to Cminor)

92

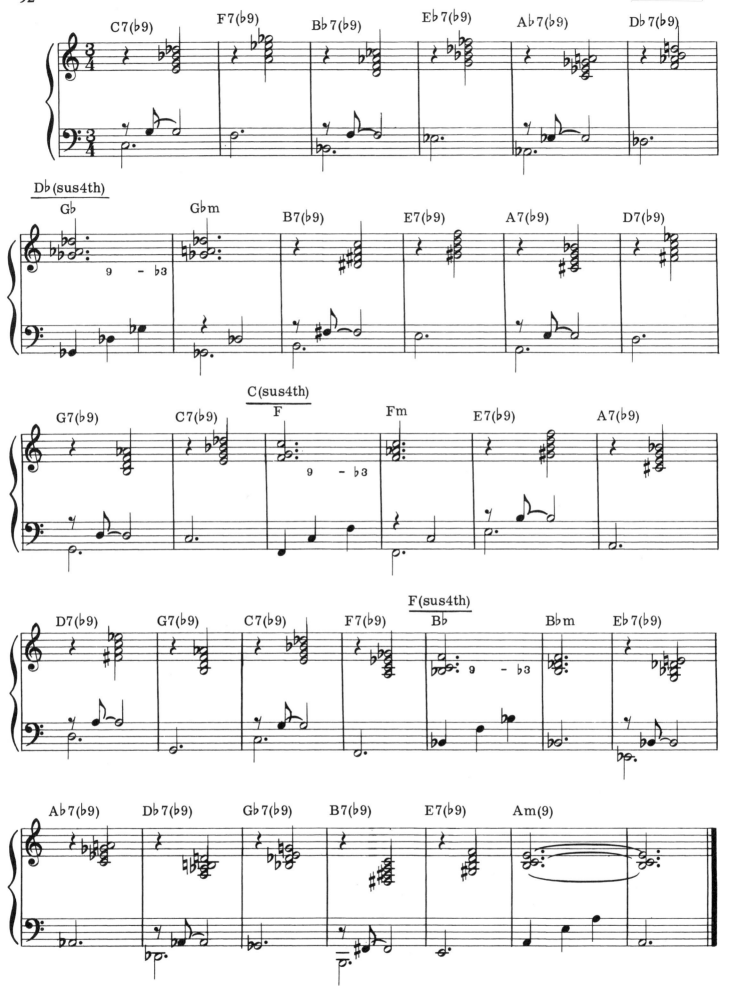

b9 - 1 RESOLUTION

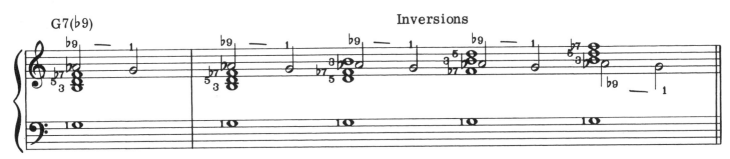

The flat 9th chord tone resolves normally to chord tone 1 (b9-1). This resolution relieves the tension created by the flat 9th.

LISTEN TO THE DIFFERENCE BETWEEN THIS SOUND:

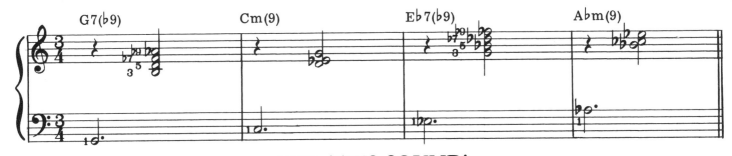

AND THIS SOUND!

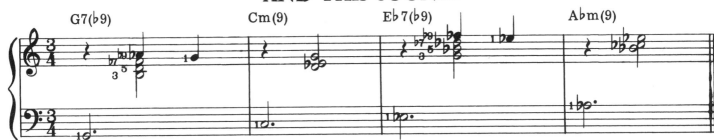

THIS SOUND:

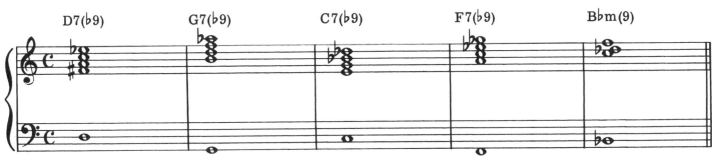

AND THIS SOUND!

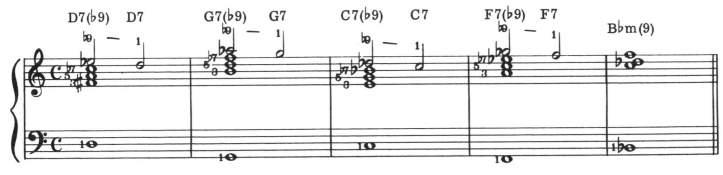

b9 - 1 INVERSIONS

b9 - 1 INVERSIONS

INVERSIONS
DOMINANT 7th, b9TH CHORDS

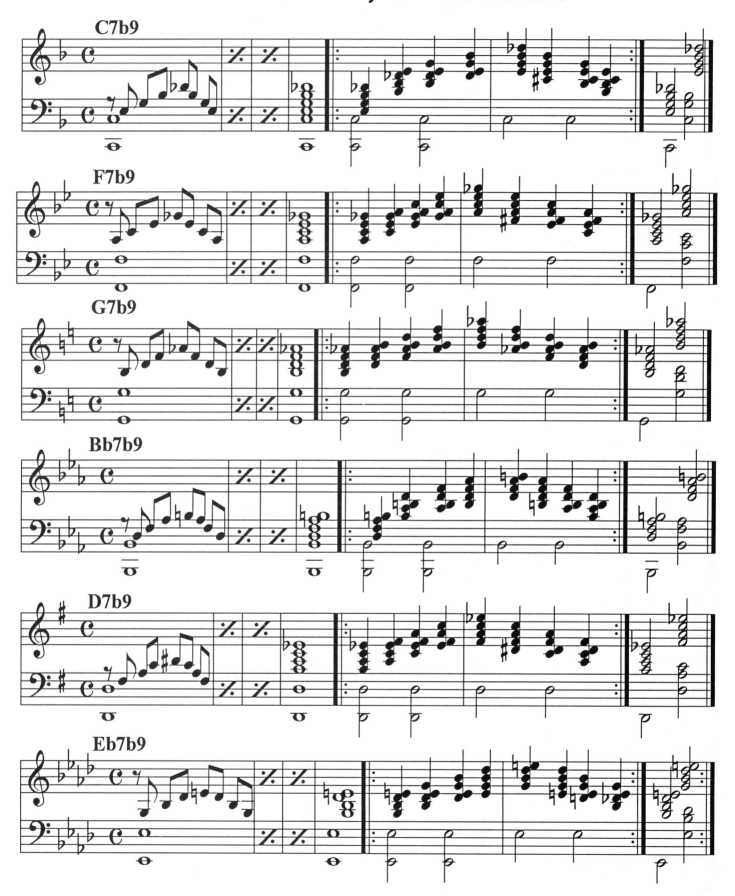

INVERSIONS
DOMINANT 7th, b9TH CHORDS

INVERSIONS
AUGMENTED 7TH WITH THE ADDED 9TH CHORDS

INVERSIONS
AUGMENTED 7TH WITH THE ADDED 9TH CHORDS

INVERSIONS
DIMINISHED 7TH WITH THE ADDED 9TH CHORDS

INVERSIONS
DIMINISHED 7TH WITH THE ADDED 9TH CHORDS

102

DOMINANT 11th CHORDS

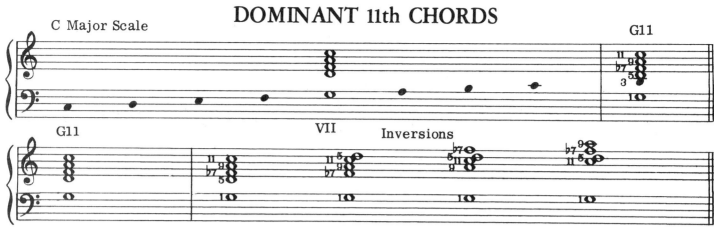

A dominant 11th chord is constructed in 3rds on the 5th note of a major scale. This is a magnificent sounding chord, especially when the 3rd is omitted. Learn it in every key.

V11 INVERSIONS

DOMINANT 11th WITH THE ADDED 13th

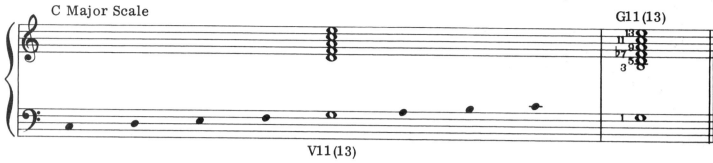

A dominant 11th with the added 13th is another beautiful sounding chord constructed on the 5th scale step of a major scale. Learn it in every key.

DOMINANT 13th CHORDS

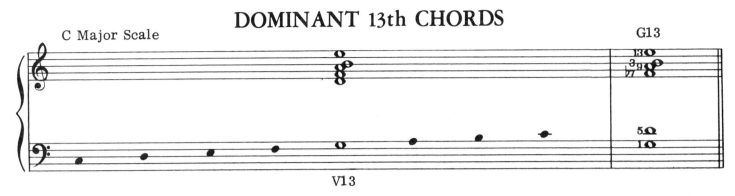

The customary voicing for a 13th chord is 13-3-9-♭7. An easy way to remember the chord tone 13th is to think of it as the 6th of a chord 13-3-9-♭7 or 6-3-9-♭7.

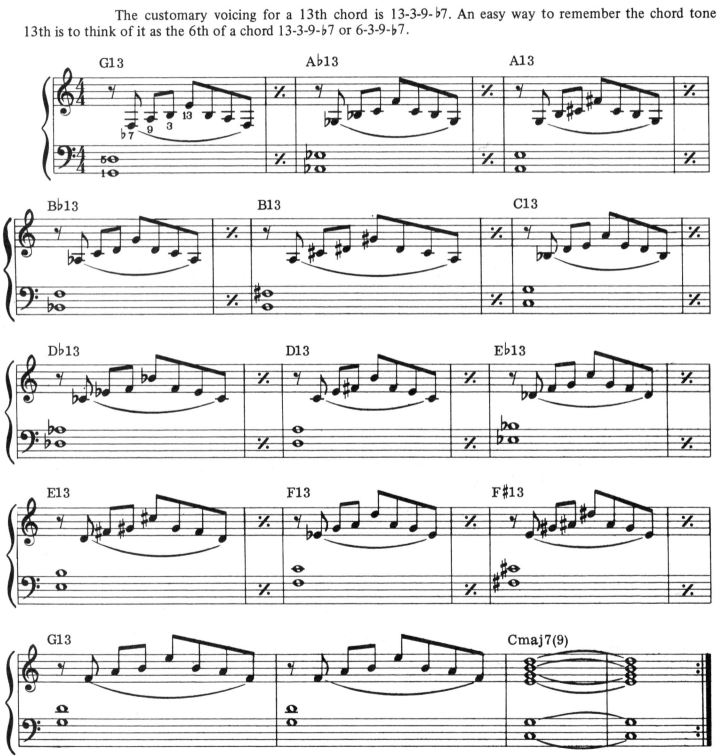

V13 EXAMPLES

*Notice in this exercise the chord tone 5th has been omitted without any apparent change in sound.

DIATONIC 11TH CHORDS

DIATONIC 11TH CHORDS

INVERSIONS
V7 FLAT 9 / 11TH CHORDS

INVERSIONS
V7 FLAT 9 / 11TH CHORDS

INVERSIONS
AUGMENTED 11TH CHORDS

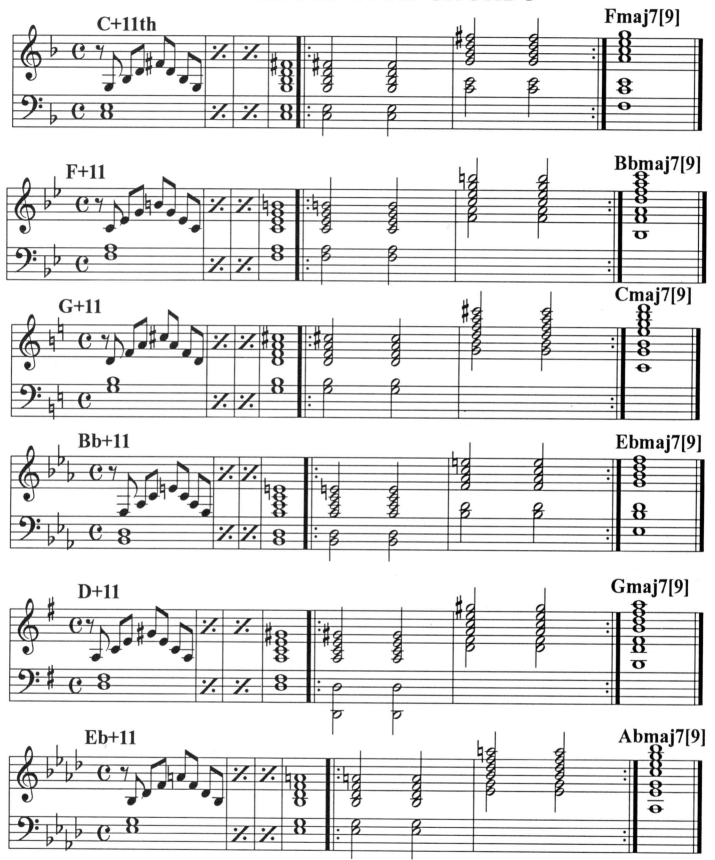

INVERSIONS
AUGMENTED 11TH CHORDS

INVERSIONS
DOMINANT 11TH WITH THE ADDED 13TH CHORDS

INVERSIONS
DOMINANT 11TH WITH THE ADDED 13TH CHORDS

INVERSIONS
AUG. 11TH/13th CHORDS

INVERSIONS
AUG. 11TH/ 13TH CHORDS

INVERSIONS
MAJOR 6TH[9] AUGMENTED 11TH

INVERSIONS
MAJOR 6TH[9] AUGMENTED 11TH

DOMINANT CHORD ALTERATIONS

When you believe you've learned and digested all of the preceding material, try practicing the following pages using these alterations:

(1)   The 5th and 9th chord tones of a dominant chord may be raised and/or lowered ½ step. G9(♯5 or ♭5) and/or (♯9 or ♭9).

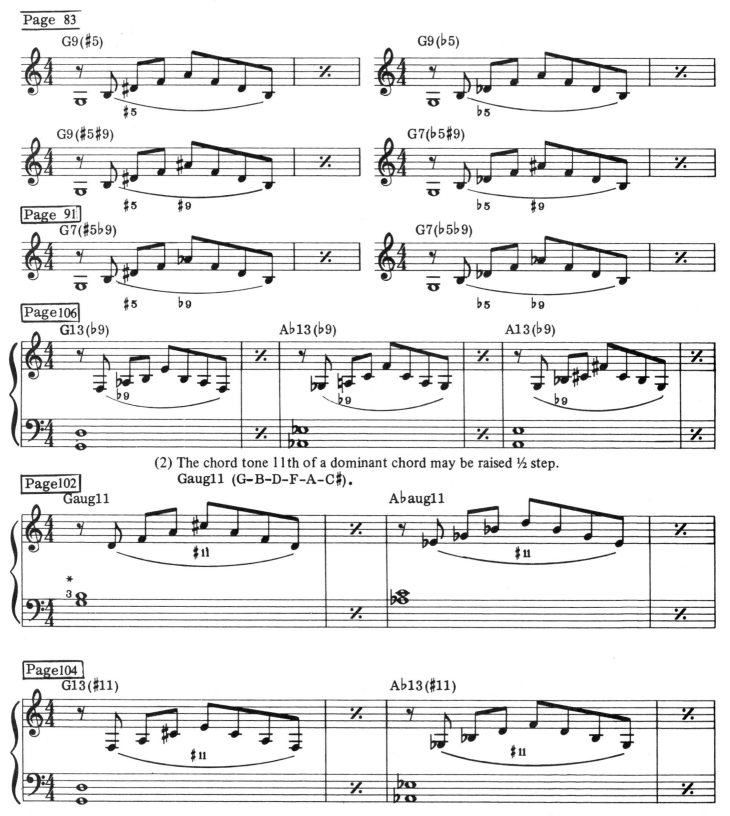

(2) The chord tone 11th of a dominant chord may be raised ½ step.
Gaug11 (G–B–D–F–A–C♯).

* Note: In this voicing, use the chord tone 3rd when playing an augmented 11 (♯11) chord.